WHAT HIDES BEHIND A GESTURE?

DAVIDE BALESI

Translation from italian to english by Giorgia Cattaneo

Copyright 2015 Davide Balesi

CONTENTS

CHAPTER 1: INTRODUCTION

My name is Davide Balesi, I am a writer and I wrote several handbooks on seduction and on psychology applied to courtship.
I consider myself an expert on interpersonal relationships. My personal background consists of many readings and of four years experience in the dynamics of social relationships among people, especially between men and women.
In the past years my poor knowledge of body language led to disappointing relationships and made me unable to establish good connections with people. How can you seduce a woman if you can't even understand what she is saying to you? How can you win a negotiation if you can't even understand which side your interlocutor is on? How can you understand people's intentions when you are not even sure if they are telling the truth?
If you rest on the meaning of words only, you belong to the 90% of male population, and like this percentage you will never be able to establish empathy with your

interlocutors.

I referred to a male percentage because women, for genetic reasons, are better readers of body language. Nature gave women this ability so that they could take care of infants that, by nature, can't use words to communicate. Women have an innate maternal instinct which allows them to establish empathy with their speakers.

Observing a group of people, a woman could understand the relationships among them in a few minutes. A man couldn't!

Therefore women, as opposed to men, have an advantage in studying body language!

Many gestures of body language are universally recognized, which means they are accepted by all cultures and thus they are more meaningful than any spoken word: a smile, for example. Other gestures are typical of a specific culture and they can have different meanings for other cultures, for example the sign of the horns.

The study of body language is a science and it must be considered as such. It's been several years since worldwide famous psychologists have started classifying body signs and studying their meanings; every psychotherapist or psychiatrist is able to understand his patient thanks to his studies on nonverbal communication.

I wanted to write this easy handbook to help you understand people, and therefore improve your social relationships. To make the subject easier, I decided to gather all the main body signs in four big groups:

☐ Man-woman relationship in seduction

☐ Personal spaces

☐ Closed and denial gestures and behaviours

☐ Positive gestures of openness and honesty

☐ Lie or truth signs

☐ Consideration gestures

☐ Exercises to test your learning

I hope that this partition will make your learning process easier.

Remember that you can easily lie with words but not with body language!

Keep in mind that 90% of communication is nonverbal! There are facial expressions, vocal variations, posture, unintentional gestures and proxemics. Words often hide the real meaning of a communication.

If you learn to read the meaning of nonverbal language you will also learn to understand yourself better. Have you ever felt uncomfortable in a situation and made a gesture or stroke an attitude unintentionally? You probably wondered about the meaning of your gestures, am I wrong? This handbook will answer all your questions!

The best salesmen were trained with specific courses about body language; they have to understand when a client is really interested in buying their product; they know when it's time to change their attitude depending on the signals that their potential buyer throws, and most of the times they can successfully close their negotiation.

Learning the basics in this field unfortunately is not enough. You have to practice to excel! So, once you have studied this handbook, try to critically observe people and focus on their body language rather than on their verbal language. You will be surprised to realize that people are often in contradiction with what they say!

When you are about to read body language you have to be consistent: you have to consider not only one gesture but a mass of gestures, and above all you have to put them in the right context. A single gesture decoded in the wrong context can lead you to the wrong meaning of the communication!

Enjoy your reading!

Davide Balesi – author of Seduction and Education –

CHAPTER 2: BODY LANGUAGE AND SEDUCTION

You can study many handbooks about seduction and you can be familiar with all kinds of approaches and all kinds of women; but if you don't know body language and its meaning, you will always have a hard time seducing people. This is true for both men and women, but especially for men, as they are incapable in courtship by nature, while women know very well-structured seduction strategies.

FOR MEN:
You can understand whether a woman is attracted or not, by studying her body language in these particular situations:

1) She makes specific gestures or takes specific attitudes towards you.

2) She uses a specific body language when you enter her range of vision.

3) She uses a specific body language when she talks to you.

If a woman likes you, she will give you one or more appreciation signs. These signals, which indicate how much she is attracted to you, are very important. If you don't notice them you will jeopardize your opportunity to seduce a woman.

You have to develop the ability of noticing the appreciation signs; but be careful, you never have to show your pursuit at the presence of a woman because she would notice it. You have to act discreetly!

You have to become perceptive!

For example, you can start observing the details when you enter a room. When you talk to a woman that you want to seduce, you have to constantly keep eye contact and at the same time study her moves, even her smallest moves.

During the years when I went through hundreds of different approaches in different places and situations, I could classify around seventeen appreciation signs of an attracted woman.

According to the numbers and kinds of noticed signals, you have to choose the most suitable approach. In my first e-book: "How to attract and seduce women with the secrets of italian latin lover" I explained all these concepts in details, and I applied them to the approaches that I reported in my second e-book: "12 Approcci vincenti". These are the body language signs that you can notice in a woman when she likes you. If you notice at least two or three of them, you can be almost sure that she is attracted to you:

1) She wants an apparently insignificant contact, like adjusting your tie or grabbing your wrist to check the time or adjusting your jacket lapel or stroking your neck:

Physical contact is a good indicator of interest, and above all you can find this indicator in almost all cultures.

But remember that not all cultures use it with the same intensity. Physical contact is generously used towards the speaker and therefore totally accepted in Latin cultures, like Italian; while it is not as frequent in Northern or Asian cultures, where it is usually more delicate. Keep this difference in mind when you are about to approach a woman from another Country. Anyway, a woman that "adjusts" your look, using gestures that are more or less intentional, is attracted to you because she cares about the way you look.

2) She shows you her hand palm and wrist, and with the other hand she strokes her hair or other body parts:

When a woman is attracted to you, she will often show you her wrist while she is talking to you, since it is an erogenous and vulnerable area; it's as if she is offering you an intimate part of her body.

Pay also attention when a woman smokes in your company; if she holds the cigarette showing you her wrist, when she is not inhaling, it means that she probably likes you.

A woman that has an interest in you will often look at you in an engaged way and at the same time she will gently wrap her hair around her finger.

Showing her wrist and wrapping her hair simultaneously indicate a strong attraction towards you.

3) The woman wants your physical contact even though she is doing something else:

For example, she is writing a text message and touching your shoulder at the same time. If she doesn't divert her attention from you it means that she likes you!
She will probably brush against your arm, elbow or shoulder. She could also fleetingly lay her hand on your chest.
She is unlikely to touch your face or hair

4) She keeps eye contact:

Looking at your interlocutor for a longer time than what courtesy requires is often a sign of interest. That's why I suggest you to use it with women that you want to attract; firstly because it shows that you are in control, and secondly because it creates a state of attraction.
Pay attention to the way she is looking at you though. If she looks at you with a furrowed brow and she focuses on the bridge of your nose, it means that she feels resentment towards you. Instead, if she starts looking down to your neck it means that she is interested.
So looks are not always the same. Even a beginner in

body language studies can obviously tell the difference between a look showing hate and one showing attraction.

5) She tends to stand close to you:

Closeness is often a sign of attraction. If you are in a club and you notice that a girl keeps coming close to you, even though she has all the space available in the room, she could be interested in you.

Closeness is not easy to interpret because you have to assess the distance she keeps from you. I would say that if she stands a metre away from you it's like if she is entering your personal space. It is your job to get to know her better and understand whether she could be interested in you. Try to look at her and she should look back at you. You could then start a conversation with a simple icebreaker.

6) She faces you while she talks to you:

If she offers you her body when she talks to you, she could be attracted. Strangers don't usually enter our personal space when they are talking to us and, above all, they are unlikely to stand exactly opposite to us. People usually adopt a three quarter defensive posture, slightly lateral towards us. People with a more dominant personality or that are more self-confident tend to be more frontal than those who are more insecure and shy.

7) The woman's pupils look dilated when she talks to you:

Pupils' dilation is a clear sign of attraction for both men and women. According to some recent studies, pupils become 4 times bigger if we are looking at something attractive and exciting
Obviously you have to keep in mind that pupils also dilate when the light is weak to allow us a better vision. Always take into consideration this natural factor.

8) She keeps looking at your lips when you talk:

Besides keeping eye contact, an attracted woman will constantly look at your lips while you talk because she consciously or unconsciously wants to kiss them. This is a strong sign of appreciation.

9) With her joined hands under her chin, she "offers" you her face so that you can admire it:

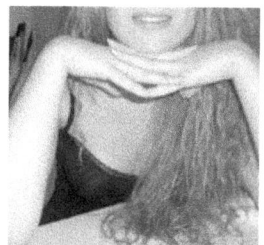

If a woman likes you, she will put her face into a hypothetical foreground that she creates with her joint hands, so that you can admire it. It's as if she said: "Do you like me? Judge my beauty because I have already judged yours and I find you interesting". This gesture is usually accompanied by a smile or a series of smiles and it is made by the woman while you are talking. For physical reasons it will be hard for her to make it when she is talking.

10) She slowly touches her body lightly:

This is a clear sign of sexual attraction towards you. Her caresses are usually short but frequent. The woman unconsciously wants to be caressed by you. Women usually touch their hips or a shoulder, sometimes their hair too. Anyway these caresses implicate attraction towards the interlocutor.

.

11) She projects her lips while she talks to look sexy:

By projecting their lips and keeping them half open,

women want to act like "femme fatale" and stimulate the sex drive of the man standing in front of them. Projected lips can be accompanied by semi-closed eyes. In collective imagination lips remind to the female sexual organ, so they are a strong sexual reference. Women are aware of this and they wear lipsticks that make their lips look bigger and turgid.

12) She plays with a phallic shaped object:

This gesture has an extremely strong connotation. Phallic shaped objects always have a strong sexual reference. A woman can play with the neck of a bottle or with a glass. Her moves are usually slow. If they play fast or nervously, they could be stressed or anxious. Check where she puts the bottle on the table: if she puts it in front of her she wants to put up barriers between you, if she puts it on a side she wants to break down barriers. Anyway, an appreciation sign is usually followed by a second one.

13) She wiggles her hips:

A woman wiggles her hips to draw your attention on her proportions. Women are aware of the attractive power that a good waist-hips ratio has and she uses this to attract men.
When hips are slightly bigger than waist, the woman is likely to have a good reproductive capacity. A bad waist-hips ratio doesn't attract men.

14) She delicately takes her shoe off, constantly:

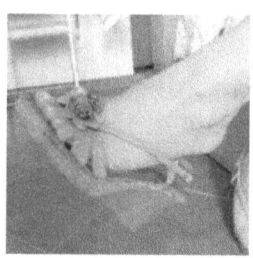

It's a gesture that an attracted woman constantly makes, and it says that she feels at ease with you. Many people see a sexual connotation in this gesture.

15) Her knee is bent under the other leg:

One leg is bent under the other. A woman usually adopts this pose when she is sitting on a couch at the presence of an interlocutor.

This is a proper indication, more than a sign. Her knee points the man she is attracted to. Furthermore, if the woman wears a skirt, she shows off her legs and this is a strong sexual reference for men

16) She constantly flips her hair:

A woman constantly flips her hair to call her interlocutor's attention on her neck. The neck is considered a very vulnerable, erogenous and intimate area because it is usually hidden by hair. By uncovering her neck, a woman offers you her vulnerability.

17) She looks and smiles at you at a distance:

When you enter the visual field of a woman that is

attracted to you, she will cursory look at you and smile. She usually stares back at you for three seconds, then she glances down and in a few seconds she will look again. These glances are a call for an approach from you. Many men can't see them because they don't look around.

Remember that a woman's invitation will never be explicit or bold; she will look at you 3 or 4 times at most. If you don't approach her soon, she will lose interest in you. Rejection signs are the opposite of appreciation signs. They are used by the woman that you are approaching, but that doesn't like you. These signs can be clear since the beginning of the conversation or they can appear during your approach, maybe because of something you did or said. Understanding these signs will help you not to waste time over a woman you made a bad impression on straight away, or to improve your behaviour so that she can change her mind about you.

You have to consider that a person gets a sense of who you are in the first seconds that you meet, maybe from a handshake. Approaching a woman with the correct body language is essential to make a first good impression on her.

Here are the 10 main rejection signs:

1) Her knees are crossed, her legs are tight and her feet are joined or her arms are crossed over her chest:

These are signs of a closed attitude of the person standing in front of us. You need to change your attitude in order to change hers.

When the arms of a woman are crossed she is building a sort of wall between herself and her interlocutor.

The same applies to crossed feet.

.

2) Her hands are joined over her stomach, or one of her hands holds her wrist tight over her breast:

This is a comfort position linked to a situation that is causing anxiety. In both cases the woman is refusing the person standing in front of her.

3) She covers her face with her hands:

This is the opposite of the situation we have seen before, where the woman offers you her face to make you admire it. In this case she is trying to hide from you. This usually means denial or refusal.

4) She holds a glass in her hand and keeps it between herself and the other person:

The glass allows the woman to build a barrier. Even when you sit at the same table and she puts a glass or a bottle in the middle of it, she wants to create a division. Always try to make a woman assume an openness position. If she is creating a barrier talking about a specific topic, stop it and think about the next move.

5) She rubs her nose horizontally:

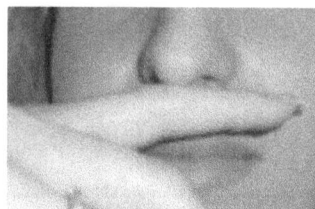

In this case she is refusing the other person's behaviour or gesture. If she rubs her nose with her index finger in a vertical movement - as if she wanted to unblock her nose and take a breath- she is expressing refusal towards her interlocutor.

6) She bites her lips and nervously moves her foot:

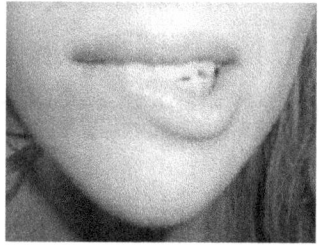

If running the tongue slowly on the lips suggests

appreciation, biting nervously at them suggests a stressful situation. The woman doesn't feel at ease in your company. Try and create more feeling with her. Try not to look threatening and always consider the audacity of what you are talking about.

7) She avoids any physical contact, also accidental ones:

I have already explained to you the meaning of a constant physical contact. If a woman pulls back when you go closer, or if she moves her hand when you try to touch it, 99% of the times she is not attracted to you. Always consider the audacity of your gestures. Starting a physical contact during the first few minutes of the conversation would make the majority of women feel uncomfortable.
Always consider her attraction towards you before starting touching her.

8) She moves one of your belongings away from her:

If you sit at a table with a woman, and you put on purpose or accidentally one of your belongings closer to her - a mobile phone for instance - and she moves it away during the conversation, that means that she wants to keep you away or that she doesn't enjoy your company. Such a gesture expresses therefore a refusal towards the interlocutor or the dining companion.

9) She wipes or brushes something off a surface:

This is an instinctive refusal of the conversation that you are listening to. The act of wiping or brushing off your clothing means that the conversation has been refused.

10) Clearing her throat:

This gesture symbolically represents the attempt of refusing or keeping a subject, a gesture, an event or a situation away.

FOR WOMEN:

Some of the rejection signs that a woman uses in order to distance a man are the same signs that a man uses to reject a woman: clearing the throat, for instance or moving an object away, and the same goes for physical contact. If a man is attracted by you he will constantly touch you

The seducing repertoire of a woman is extensive; on the contrary, the appreciation signs of an attracted man are not so many, and they are easy to decode.

90% of men are incapable of seducing, firstly because they don't know the articulate art of seduction; secondly because they are more rational and less emotional, so they go straight to the point.

This difference can be often recognised in the way a man and a woman talk about an experience they have lived. A woman will use colourful words and she will go into details, but above all she will always talk about the feelings she had when she lived that experience. The story of a man is often more concise, with less details, but above all, he will avoid talking about how he felt. This difference is traceable in male and female seduction.

A man will usually flaunt his status to seduce you. If he has a great car he will do anything to inform you about it; if he is successful with women he will have you read that between the lines; if he has a nice body he will try to show you his muscles as much as possible. The way men think is basically correct because women are very attracted by their status and they usually choose the man that excels in specific fields: the famous sportsman, the richest, the most handsome, the playboy.

The most common mistake that a man does during seduction is approaching a woman immediately, showing his interest straight away.

A seducer will always wait for a sign of appreciation before showing you his interest.

A seducer is able to keep a woman in a constant state of curiosity because he makes himself look interesting, out of reach and hard to seduce. A seducer will make a woman ask herself: "Who is this man that doesn't fall for me? Why doesn't he need me like the others do?"

The majority of men will beg for your attention and, as you women know well, this makes you feel less attracted. Moreover, the majority of men aren't self-confident or they show a fake self-confidence that every woman is able to unmask easily.

The majority of "brave" men will approach you directly, asking your name or offering you a drink. Has it ever happened to you to be in a club and realize that men's approaches are all the same? This causes annoyance and disgust in a woman, not attraction.

Usually, a "normal" man meet you in this way:

- not very smart in his look, or badly dressed- Not very

nice;

- with poor culture and dialectic;

- he uses unoriginal and ordinary approaches;

- he has an excessive need of attention;

- not very proactive;

- dominated by other people's decisions;

- not very empathic;

- he talks about boring subjects;

- not very ambitious;

- he talks about other people and tries to denigrate them to show you he is worthy;

This is how a seducer will look:

- smart in his look and clothing;

- he approaches you in an original way;

- educated and with gift of gab;

- very empathic because he knows body language;

- he talks about feelings;

- he is a leader and he is very ambitious;

- he is very proactive;

- he talks about feelings and not about people;

  he never denigrates people, on the contrary he helps
them;

- he never begs for your attention;

- his time is very precious;

- he is very self-confident;

- he is charming and gets the attention of everybody.

I bet I have just portrayed your ideal man, haven't I?
A woman can hardly resist such a man, even though he is not good looking or rich.
Beauty isn't just appearance for a woman.

These are the main body signs that you will notice in an attracted man:

1- He tries to have a constant physical contact:
The attracted man will start touching you soon after you met but above all, he will try to have a physical contact, accidentally at first and then clearly. For instance, he will put his hand around your waist to hug you shortly, or he

will try to stroke your hair

2- He shows his muscles:

For instance, he can put his hand behind his neck to show you his biceps. Some men also put both hands.

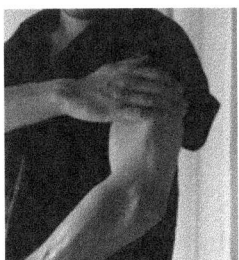

He can roll up his sleeves and briefly fondles his biceps when he is talking to you. Men with nice bodies and a little narcissist will use these postures more than other men that are less attractive.

3- He hooks his thumbs in to his belt:

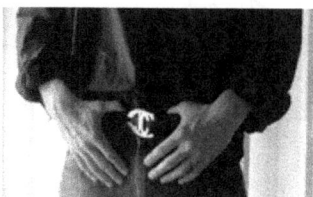

This position enhances the virility of a man. The fingers indicate the genital area and they draw attention to it. A man who adopts this posture wants to emphasize his leading and self-confident side and a clear interest in you.

4- He repeatedly looks and smiles at you:

When a man likes you, he will constantly look at you. His glances won't be veiled but very clear, almost intrusive. He will repeatedly look at your face, your breasts and especially at your bum.

When you look back at him he will make a long smile or a series of smiles.

5- He looks at you in the eyes and keeps lowering his gaze towards your neckline:

A man's sexual arousal is purely based on sight; therefore he will look at your neckline a few times. While you are talking about your last holidays, he is already imagining he is caressing and kissing your breasts. If you want to unmask him, ask him a detail about what you have just said: he won't remember.

6- He keeps looking at your lips while you are talking:

Lips are a strong sexual reference for a man. A man who constantly looks at your lips longs to kiss you. You can also notice that he will slowly get closer to your face and this is usually the beginning of a kiss.

7- He keeps a strong and constant eye contact:

An attracted man will never glances down during a conversation with you, unless he is very shy. His eye contact will be strong and persistent.

.8) His pupils dilate:

Like women's pupils, men's pupils dilate as well when they look at something attractive.

In conclusion: women, you should try and understand that a man's approach is often cold and direct. Men, you should try and understand that seducing a woman is something very articulate and veiled.

In the last few years there has been an increasing number of single people like never before.

Men and women are not able to communicate with one another in the real world.

Women dream of ideal men that are out of reach and men are frustrated because of the constant rejections they get from women.

A lot of men have become shy because of their constant failures; their self-confidence has been influenced by women's repeated rejections.

Women are often influenced by the prototype of man that the media offer. Extremely beautiful, rich and famous individuals are hard to find and they don't represent the majority of male population anyway. I never say to a woman to content herself with what she has, on the contrary, she should always aim for the best partner that she can have.

I just say that shy men should have a possibility too, because it may take longer for them to show they are worthy.

I have always said to men to improve their look and to try and understand the emotional side of women.

Different views often bring to incomprehension between sexes.

It's easier for women to obtain sex and, ironically, they seek it less than men.

Men, that instead want to have sex always and unselfishly, obtain it with more difficulty.

Men: study women's behaviours and their meanings.
Women: try to understand the logical behaviours of

men.

As you have just read in this chapter, body always says more than words in courting. This goes also and especially for courting made by women.
When you enter a crowded room try to understand if people are using body language to communicate their interest in you. Always practice your observation skills.

CHAPTER 3: PERSONAL SPACES

Have you ever felt uncomfortable or have you ever kept a distance when a stranger got too close to you? Have you ever noticed someone withdrawing from you while you are talking too close to them? I imagine this has happened to you more than once. There is an imaginary space called Personal Space around each person. The size of this space depends on the personality, culture and environment of the person. There are two kinds of personal space: large and small. In the large personal space we can let the majority of strangers in, without feeling bothered. In the small personal space, only some close people can get in: relatives, close friends, partners, masseurs, doctors, etc.

LARGE SPACE: (up to 3 metres)

SMALL SPACE: (up to 50 cm)

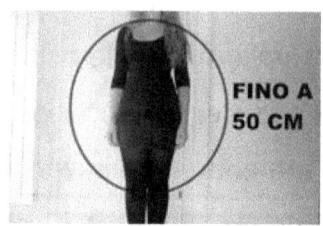

The size of the personal space area is very personal. It's bigger in Northern and Asian Countries and in those communities with few citizens, where it can get up to two metres. People that are used to live in densely populated cities know that the environment around them doesn't allow big personal spaces.

In few tiny mountain communities with maybe 20/30 inhabitants, the extended space, where strangers are accepted, can even reach four metres.

Have you ever felt uncomfortable in very crowded spaces? When strangers enter our small personal space we feel uncomfortable, as if someone was violating our "private property".

People that are more willing to give and receive physical

contact will have both the large and the small personal space more reduced than shy and introverted people. Always pay attention to how close you get to your interlocutors. If you notice that they withdraw or lean back when you go closer, try to make a step away from them. You can't establish a dialogue that is worthwhile if one of the interlocutors feels uncomfortable. Salesmen know it very well and they always look for an approval body signal first, before they approach their potential client, assuming a confidential behaviour. A house is a personal space too and in fact, if a stranger comes in without our explicit approval, we feel extremely uncomfortable. To give you an idea of how big personal spaces are, look at the following pictures.

LARGE SPACE OF AN EXTROVERTED PERSON: (up to 2-3metres)

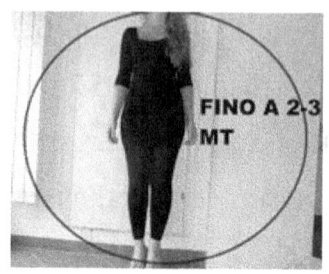

LARGE SPACE OF AN INTROVERTED PERSON: (up to 3-4 metres)

SMALL SPACE OF AN EXTROVERTED PERSON: (up to 10-20 cm)

SMALL SPACE OF AN INTROVERTED PERSON: (up to 20-30 cm)

You can have an idea of the personal space of the person you have just met by shaking their hand: people that need more space will stay far from the interlocutor, and they will stretch their arm to make the gesture, the arm will be almost completely stretched out:

People that need less space will stay closer to the interlocutor and they will bend their arm:

In order not to make people feel uncomfortable try a gradual approach.

Above all, use a lot of friendly gestures - we will go through them in the next chapters - and smile. A smile makes us look friendly and not dangerous and it helps us to establish a peaceful interpersonal relationship. If you notice that you have invaded their space too much, step back and try to adopt openness gestures and positions. Don't force the personal space of very shy people: a few minutes conversation is not enough to do that, you have to know this person better first.

Suppose you are a door to door encyclopaedia salesman and that you are about to go into a potential customer's house. Your goal is to obtain a confidential proximity with your customer; therefore you have to make him trust you unconditionally. Introduce yourself while you are still on his doorstep; in order not to invade his space, shake his hand while saying your name and smile, then explain what you are selling. Try to show often your hand palms while you talk, because this is a gesture that indicates openness and honesty, then consider your customer's reaction: if he adopts a closure position -crossed arms or legs- you have to approach him again trying to be more persuasive.

If your customer shows you that he is sociable and he doesn't put up barriers, you can slowly start to get closer and you can ask permission to go into his house to explain your selling reasoning better.

The more persuasive you are and the more honest you look, the more likely your client is to let you get closer. Once you are close to him you can try a soft physical contact by fleetingly touching his elbow: this gesture will help him trust you more. When you are near his constricted space, you will have good chances to successfully close the deal.

If you continue your negotiation around a table, the host will give you a seat creating a debate position, which means opposite to him with a barrier that is represented by the table.

Look at the following picture. You are A, and your client is B:

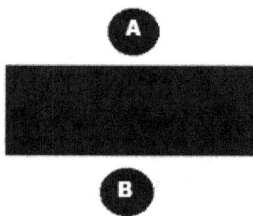

This is a typical debating position. In such a context there is no physical contact and there is a big barrier between you.

Every persuasion and openness attempt can turn out to be vain because of the barrier represented by the table. Your goal is to switch from a debating position to a closeness position, which means that you should move to the side of the table where your client is, and sit close to him:

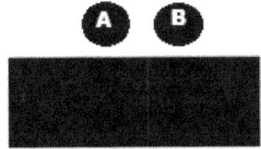

Your goal is to switch from a debating position to a closeness position, which means that you should move to the side of the table where your client is, and sit close to him.

For example, showing your client your catalogue could be an opportunity to get to this position. This friendly position allows you to establish an equal relationship, and above all, a collaboration relationship in a friendly environment.

If your potential client feels at ease you have more chances to sell your products.

Suppose you are about to approach a stranger in a club. His/her personal space is already constricted because of the number of people in that place. Always smile in a genuine way so that people don't consider you as a threat.

For men: approach a woman facing her, so that she can see you and check you from a distance, and when you go near a man, do it always from a side so that he doesn't consider the approach as a provocation.

For women: you can approach a man from a side or facing him, never approach people from behind. Every individual has to have the opportunity to see you, before you start any kind of approach. Rationing physical contact is essential if you don't want to come across as intrusive: try with some gently touches that have to seem accidental, and then go on with clearer touches.

Men, you must know that a lot of women don't want to have their hair touched, because they have spent hours to get ready and look perfect before going out.
Women, you must know that some men don't want their cheeks to be touched, because they would feel childish.
In any case, if you manage to enter a person's constricted space, it's a done deal. It's very important to establish an environment where your interlocutor feels relaxed and at ease, in order to build an interpersonal relationship.

CHAPTER 4: REJECTION AND AUTHORITY GESTURES

When a person doesn't feel at ease with you or they don't want to talk to you, they will assume a body language that indicates closure, which means rejection. I decided to describe rejection and authority gestures in the same chapter for a simple reason: if we give orders or say something in a pose that looks commanding, we can raise a negative feeling in our interlocutor, bringing them to close. This depends on our status compared to theirs. I make an example to give you a better idea. Let's say that you are head of production and you are giving an order to one of your workers: if you adopt a dominant pose, they will accept the situation and the order; but if you give orders with the same pose to another head of production, they could get annoyed by feeling your dominant state. If a body language that expresses lack of openness always has a negative connotation, the one that expresses authority can produce different results, depending on the situation.

CLOSED BODY LANGUAGE:

Hands in pockets: they indicate that the person doesn't want to talk and communicate; that's because the person is hiding the palms that instead are usually used during a conversation. This closed gesture is usually used by shy and introverted people that don't like to be the centre of attention.

If you want to avoid an unwanted conversation, put your hands in your pockets so that your interlocutor can understand that you don't want to communicate. Anyway, I always suggest never using any closed gestures. If you approach a person always show your palms, or you will irritate them; and if you want to be approached, always avoid hiding your hands.

The hand in pockets position with thumbs out has a totally different and opposite meaning - we will see it in the next chapter-.

Arms and/or legs crossed: nothing is clearer than this posture. Closing your arms over your chest or crossing your ankles indicates total closure and rejection towards both the conversation and the interlocutor. The person adopting this posture wants to create a defensive barrier, in order not to be approached..

A lot of people adopt this defensive pose when they feel insecure in specific contexts, such as:
- waiting in a clinic before a medical examination;
- talking to an unpleasant person;

- talking to a person that is lecturing us;
- when they are in a very crowded place;
- when they feel observed or at the centre of attention.

Basically in every situation that causes uncertainty or discomfort. Introverted people will show it more than extroverted people. Suppose you are approaching a stranger in a night club. If this person crosses their arms straight away at the beginning of the conversation, it means that you either started it in the wrong way, or that this person doesn't want to be bothered; you can test the water by trying to create a friendly environment - using openness gestures - while you talk If you notice that your interlocutor uncrosses their arms, you can continue the approach, otherwise you better leave. If instead, the person shows openness at the beginning -hands in sight and no barriers- and afterwards they adopt a closure position, you may have said or done something wrong: change subject or attitude, and consider their following signals.

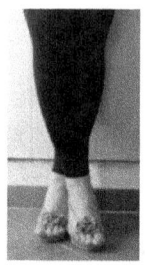

Crossed ankles usually go with folded arms and they intensify their meaning. A lot of people say that they fold their arms because they feel at ease: this is partly true, because it's a defensive position that allows building a barrier between you and whatever is causing your discomfort. Never fold your arms because you could irritate the majority of people.

Arms crossed with grip: a variation of folded arms is the same position with triceps grasp.

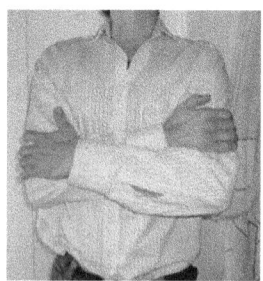

The grasp indicates an anxious feeling that we are trying to control, an attempt to vent our frustration by holding our triceps tight.

Crossed arms with clenched fists: it indicates repressed rage, as well as closure and rejection.
If a person adopts this position with you, it means that you have probably offended them with a gesture or a conversation. Try to understand the reason of their hostility and fix the situation.

One crossed arm: this is another closure position, where an arm grabs the other which is kept stretched on the side. Although this is a partial closed gesture, it still indicates a defensive attitude.

If you approach a woman and she adopts this position, you are not making her feel at ease; maybe you were too close and invaded her personal space. Try to step back and keep your distance.

Men are unlikely to adopt this position.

Holding a physical barrier near the body: the barrier can be represented by anything: a glass, a bottle, an umbrella, and a purse (by women).

This position can also be adopted when you are at a table. For example, a woman could place her purse between you.

Insecure people feel at ease by placing an object between them and the surrounding environment.

As long as the interlocutor keeps their barrier up, every attempt you make to "open" them will be vain.

If you are sitting at a table in a debating position (chapter 3), your interlocutor is more likely to place a barrier. In a more confidential position, it would be harder for him to make this gesture.

People often imitate our gestures. When you are sitting at a table, never place an object between you and your interlocutor, or you will irritate them and you will bring them to create a barrier.

Motor synchronization, that is imitating the other person's gestures, usually happens between people that feel attracted to each other. So, first of all, pay attention to what your attitude is towards people.

Joined hands at groin height: this is typical of those people who feel insecure in a specific environment. Hands are joined and lowered at groin height.
This position indicates closure that, for example, could be caused by a strong emotional state, or by a very stressful situation.
Think about a not very charming public speaker that has to talk in front of many people.

.

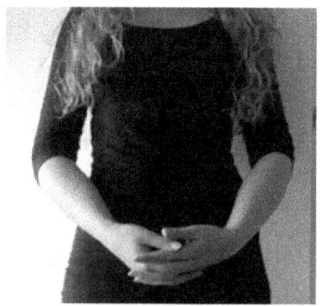

Joined hands over face: this position is adopted by anxious and insecure people. Fingers are strongly intersected, and hands are usually placed at face height, in an attempt to hide it.

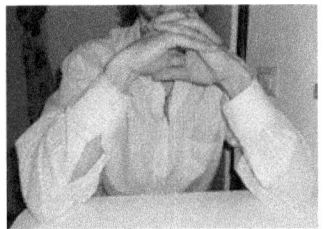

This position is adopted in situations that cause discomfort.

When a person approaches someone of the opposite sex, and they realize that this person is not interested, they usually adopt the intersected hands gesture, irritating the other person even more and showing all their insecurity. This pose should always be avoided in favour of others that show self-confidence (chapter 5).

Weak handshake: A simple handshake can be a negative sign too, that indicates closure and insecurity. A typical handshake is the one with no strength, in this case our hand will be squeezed by a dominant and confident opposite party - a man most of the times - but above all, it will always be perceived as the indicator of an unconfident and easily influenced personality.

When you are about to shake someone else's hand, make sure you do it with a slight strength, enough to make the other person feel your hand.

Avoid a too strong handshake, and avoid shaking your interlocutor's hand too much.

If you are a man and you are shaking a woman's hand you have to use a faint but perceptible strength.

Men can use a stronger handshake among them.

Women, you should try to have a strong handshake if you don't want to come across as weak and insecure.

Finally, always remember to smile and look at the other person in the eye when you shake their hand. There is nothing more annoying than a person looking at the floor, or worst at the hands.

Avoiding your interlocutor's look: if you don't look your interlocutor in the eyes, you will come across as shy, rude, and unworthy.

This applies in all fields, but especially in seduction.

If you look the person you are approaching in the eyes, you will look confident and attractive; shy people lower their glance when people talk to them, but not you. You have to look people in the eyes!

Looking the person you are talking to in the eyes is considered sexy. The pleasure of eye contact is a feature of seduction; but if you find it embarrassing, try focusing on something else, so that you give the idea of looking in the eye, but never lower your glance and avoid bending your head.

Scratching the back of the neck: scratching the back of your neck and looking at the floor at the same time will make you look miserable or frightened.
In effect, people that are feeling negative adopt this position. For example, think about people that are told off when they know they are wrong.

Adjusting your watch or bracelet: have you ever felt observed in a club and you started adjusting your wrist watch?

This is another gesture that shows insecurity. If you touch your left wrist with your right hand, you create a barrier in front of your body.

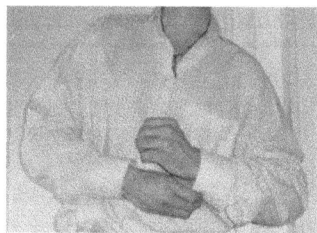

We usually adjust our watch, our bracelet, a ring, or we play with the buttons of our cuffs. This is how insecure people give vent to their discomfort.

To avoid looking insecure, you should do some practice in bearing social pressure. In a club for example, you could walk across the dance floor at the beginning of the evening, when it's empty. When everybody is sitting on the couches, you walk across the dance floor: everybody will look at you and you have to try and look determined, don't cross your arms, and don't look at the floor. It's not easy to bear social pressure, but if you practice you can achieve great results!

Sitting with crossed legs: when a person is sitting with their legs crossed, and sometimes with their arms

crossed too, they are refusing the conversation.

Crossing legs and arms expresses a total closed attitude. If you approach a person seated in that way, you are likely to receive elusive answers that are aimed to distance you.

Also in this case, it is appropriate not to look intrusive and to try and unblock a closed situation showing your palms while you talk.

When you approach someone that is seated, you should never kneel down, or you will diminish yourself. Talk to the person staying close to them but always stay upright.

On the other hand, never adopt a dominant position if you don't want to irritate them.

Keeping your head bowed: people that keep their head bowed and their chin low usually have a critical attitude towards what they are listening to or observing.
If you notice that your interlocutor is adopting this pose, try and understand the reasons of their hostility.
When the person raises their chin, the closure situation will unblock immediately.

A foot doesn't point the interlocutor: when you talk to a person, look at their feet. If one of them points outwards, your interlocutor wants to leave.

.

If one foot points you, it means that your interlocutor could find you interesting or they are appreciating the conversation. People that want to leave usually point their feet towards some possible exits. You could also notice that they are leaning back, which means that they want to leave.

The seating position of someone that wants to leave: when your interlocutor is seated but you notice that they are leaning forward, they probably want to end the conversation and leave. It's hard to persuade someone in this position because it means that they really want to leave. So, end the conversation and leave.

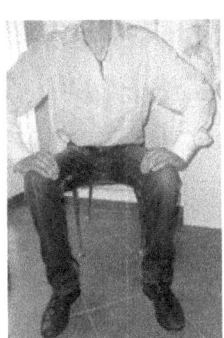

Dominant body language:

As I have explained before, not all the positions that express domination are negative, but they have to be used in the right context. Palms facing downwards: it is essential to know the meaning of hands positions for a better understanding of body language. People often gesticulate while they talk, and they direct their hands to express their concepts better. You should always look at the hand palms and see whether they are oriented upwards or downwards. If they are oriented downwards, they usually indicate authority and dominance. Let's think, for example, about a supervisor that gives an order to a subordinate: the supervisor's palms will always be down. Handshake with palm down: this is typical of dominant personalities that squeeze their interlocutor's hand, and they force them to turn their hand palm up.

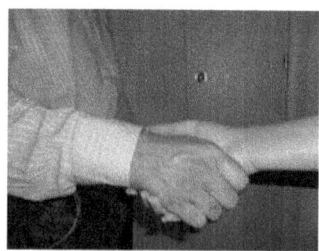

If you don't want to look submissive in front of this kind of handshake, try to slightly turn the other person's palm upwards. This handshake is mainly used by men, never used by women, and seldom used between a man and a woman.

Hands behind the back: in this position both hands are behind the back, and one hand grabs the other by the palm.

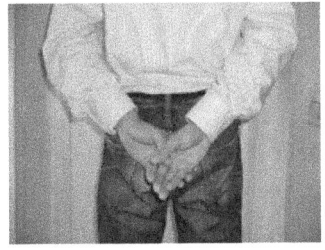

This position is adopted by people that use authority in a specific place, or that feel very confident. For example, the office manager that controls his employee's job by walking through the desks usually puts his hands behind his back. In this way you are confirming your authority.

Keeping thumbs in sight: have you ever noticed that some people keep their hands in their pockets but their thumbs are in sight while they talk to you? These people are very self-confident and tend to dominate.

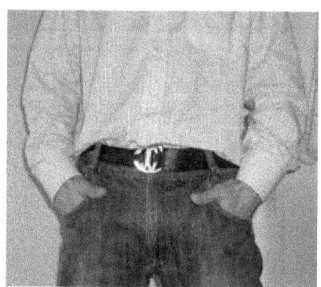

Adopt the same position or another dominant position if you want to answer their exhibited superiority.

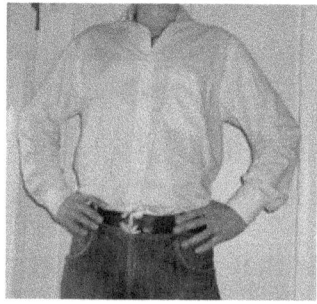

Hands on hips: this position expresses dominance. People adopting this position want to mark their territory and therefore discourage whoever has bad intentions.

Very self-confident and dominant people adopt it often. Adopt this position whenever you need to express your status.

CHAPTER 5: OPENNESS GESTURES

Openness gestures and positions are all those body signs that are beneficial to people both adopting and receiving them.

A body language that makes us appear kind and honest puts our interlocutor in the same feeling, and it creates a positive and equal interpersonal relationship.

A smile is one of these openness gestures.

As I have already explained in the previous chapters, a smile produces positive feelings to people that receive it. For example, think about when a stranger smiles at us in the street and we smile back.

Smiling makes a person kind and friendly: if this is how others perceive us, they will be more sociable with us. According to many scientific studies, smiling makes us more charming. When you are about to approach a stranger, you should try doing it with a smile on your face.

There are different ways of smiling though. The only smile that looks sincere is the total one, which involves lips and eyes as well.

A fake smile, instead, is perceived in a negative way by the majority of people. Think about a smile that involves lips only, or an asymmetric smile, which involves only one side of the lips, or a tight-lipped smile. All these ways of smiling have a negative connotation.

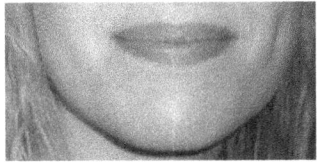

Smiling with our head tilted to one side makes us harmless to other people's eyes. Showing a vulnerable part like our neck is a submission sign.

Be ready to smile whenever the situation requires it.

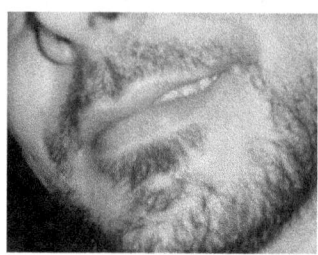

Hand palms in sight: showing our hand palms means that we have nothing to hide.

It's very important that we use this openness sign when we want to convince our interlocutor with our arguments: for example, think about a salesman that wants to persuade his client.

If you approach a stranger in a club, and you manage to look nice and interesting, you notice that they will start showing their palms gradually while they talk.

Showing palms is an involuntary gesture, which is why it is very meaningful.

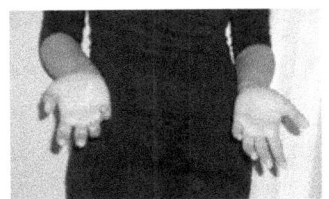

Suppose you have a job interview. Openness gestures will be very useful in this context. When your interviewer asks something like: "Are you ready to fully commit to this company?",you will answer showing your palms and saying: "You have my total commitment!". In this way you emphasize what you have just said with words. I would like to remind you that if verbal and nonverbal communications correspond, the chances you have to convince other people are high.

Joined hands like in a prayer: this position is adopted by joining hands like during a prayer; thumbs can touch the index finger or be upright. Hands can be at chest or waist height.

People with a great self-confidence often adopt this position. People that are sure they have an answer in a speech usually adopt this position.

You can use this gesture during a business meeting: if you adopt this position while other people speak, they will have the feeling that you have the right answer. Keep your hands joined even after you start speaking.

Using the right physical contact to persuade: as I have already explained, a physical contact creates a temporary but strong feeling with a person. The important thing is that you are able to control it!

You can brush your interlocutor's arm if you want to obtain something from them; you can do that only if the other person already trusts you, or you will obtain the opposite result.

Here is how men could continue their physical contact, and how this will lead them to kiss a woman in a short time:

Example of escalation:

Light/medium/intense contact:

Approach

General conversation (for example, you could ask her to show you her ring as an excuse to touch her hand – *light contact*)

General conversation but after a while (you can put your hand around her hips – *medium contact*)

If she is attracted:

strong eye contact, strong empathy (you can brush her

hair – *intense contact)*

This is a simplified progression of moves that could easily lead you to kiss a woman.

Avoid frontal positions: a frontal position is often read as a challenge/provocation, especially among men. Before you become confidential with your interlocutor, you should stand at a 45-degree angle towards them, so that you make clear that you are not a threat.

The best posture: upright, chest out and straight shoulders. This is the best pose that you can adopt.

Avoid rounded shoulders and the kyphotic posture, or you will come across as insecure and fearful.

When you walk, think about an imaginary string that pulls you up. Take big and confident steps, and you will always look self-confident.

Try walking slowly, don't rush.

You could do some sit-ups to improve your posture, because abdominals are the erector muscles of the body.

For men: try to keep your muscles toned, this will help you keep your shoulders straight and chest out.

Many people often adopt a kyphotic posture with rounded shoulder because their pectorals are more trained than their back muscles.

If you go to the gym try increasing the LAT Machine, or the pull-up exercises, in order to develop back muscles, and try to limit Pectoral Machine or push-ups exercises.

For women: if you want to improve your waist-hips ratio, try wearing high heels shoes that will make your hips sway and look sexy. Try to keep all your body muscles toned.

Do some stretching to keep your muscles flexible.

Train your gluteus doing some Squat and lunges exercises without weights.

CHAPTER 6: FIND OUT WHO IS LYING AND WHO IS TELLING THE TRUTH

Since ancient times, man has always looked for an infallible way of recognizing who was telling the truth and who was lying. He hasn't managed to do that yet! In Medieval times, adulteresses had to undergo the wrist-pulse test: the inquisitor used to repeat the name of the probable lover many times, monitoring the women's heartbeat variations, keeping his fingers on the women's wrist.

In ancient times, Chinese people used the "rice test". They used to put a handful of uncooked rice in the mouth of the investigated person, then they would ask them a question to check whether they were lying or not; after that, they used to take the rice out of their mouth, and if it was wet the person was telling the truth, if it was dry the person was lying. This unreliable method was based on the theory that emotional stress caused by a lie significantly reduces a person's saliva. Both methods were obviously scientifically unreliable! As unreliable was the use of the truth machine used by the American government.

This is how the polygraph adopted by the American legal system worked: they used to record the accused person's physiological parameters, like blood pressure, heartbeat and breathing at rest; then they used to ask them ten questions, some of them were neutral and others aimed at finding the truth. If they noticed a meaningful variation in their physiological parameters, they could presume that the accused was lying. Years after this machine was invented, they stopped considering it a reliable proof in courts.

Telling a lie gives the impostor some emotional stress, so you actually have a variation in their physiological parameters; but the machine controlling this variation doesn't recognise an easily emotional person from a person with a lot of self control. There is also a category of people who are convinced of their own lies, and that are relaxed in telling them. The truth machine used to fail with this category of people!

Thanks to the first studies on body language, we realised

a very important thing: if someone is lying, they will involuntarily adopt specific poses or gestures. Also professional liars can't control small involuntary gestures of their facial muscles.

That's why a person that understands body language well, and that is a good observer, will be able to identify the majority of liars.

Let's start identifying the first 3 categories:

The ordinary impostor: they don't know body language at all. They get usually unmasked by the majority of women - that are more capable of reading body language - and by a good percentage of men.

The ordinary impostor adopts the following postures and/or facial expressions while they lie.

- tense facial muscles;

- they touch their eyes with a finger;

- they rub their earlobe;

- they scratch the back of their neck;

- they don't look their interlocutor in the eyes;

- they hide their hand palms;

- they put their fingers in their mouth.

The expert impostor: They lie as a profession, or they just enjoy lying. Either way, they practiced to succeed in their intent, and they can hide most of body signs that indicate a lie. A good percentage of women are able to perceive the trick, most of men believe the lie instead!

The expert impostor tries to adopt an open body language, showing you their hand palms. They always keep eye contact; they never bring their hands close to their face and they often smile.
People telling lies usually don't smile, and the expert impostor knows that!
You can tell whether the expert impostor is lying only from the involuntary contractions of their facial muscles; for example, their smile could turn into a grin for a second.
When you are in front of such a person, study his lips carefully, which is where you will find the truth.

The truth teller: their facial muscles are relaxed; they

always show their palms and keep eye contact. The difference between an expert impostor and a truth teller is in the facial micro expressions caused by involuntary contractions.

Here are the main body signs indicating that a person is lying:

Fingers in mouth: most of the times, when someone brings their hands close to their face, it means that they feel under pressure. When a person puts their fingers in their mouth, they are showing their discomfort and that they are probably lying

Bringing a finger close to our lips is a reference to our childhood; it indicates that we need certainties, and that we want to get rid of a state of emotional tension.

Touching one eye: a person that rubs their eye wants to escape from a situation that is causing them anxiety, and by touching their eye they are trying to repress something or someone's sight.

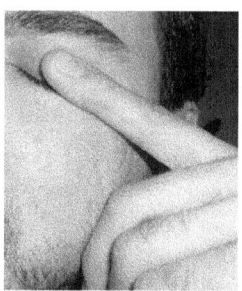

In case of an impostor, this could indicate that they want to hide from their interlocutor's eyes because they are conscious of their lie and of the possible negative effect it could have.

Scratching one's neck: scratching the neck with a finger indicates a state of uncertainty.

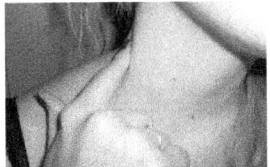

The impostor, who is conscious of telling a lie, scratches their neck and by doing that they show their insecurity.

Rubbing one's ear: someone that doesn't want to hear a conversation usually rubs their earlobe with their thumb and index finger.

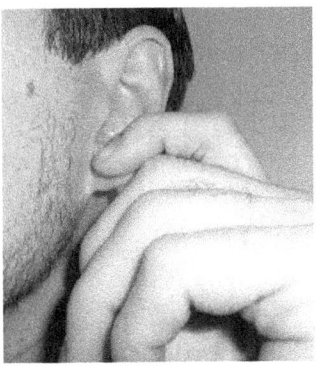

An impostor usually does that not to "hear" his lie, and they believe that their interlocutor won't pay attention to it.

Adjusting one's shirt collar: a lie puts the impostor in an anxious state and it brings them to adjust their collar as if they needed to breathe better.

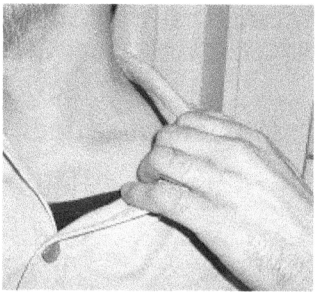

The emotional state caused by telling a lie can produce a higher level of sweat in the neck area. This explains why the impostor tries to "get some air" by moving his collar

In conclusion: women are more able than men to recognize a lie thanks to their ability at reading body language and facial expressions.
It's very hard for a man to lie to a woman, and he is very likely to be discovered. It's easier for a woman to

lie to a man, without being discovered.

As I have already explained, because of involuntary facial expressions and in front of a good observer you can't lie without being discovered. If you want to lie you should do it by writing, with a text message for example. When you lie in front of a person there will always be some factors that you can't control.

CHAPTER 7: CONSIDERATION GESTURES

Meditation or consideration gestures are all those positions that a person adopts when they are thinking about an opportunity, or when they have to make a decision. Recognizing these gestures is very useful for salespersons for instance, so that they can understand their client's intentions. In seduction, they will help you predict the answer to your request. The main consideration gestures are represented by the hands that move close to the face. Let's see them in details.

Hand on cheek to hold head: the hand palm is leaned against the cheek to support the head.

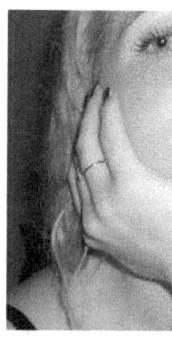

The head is usually bent towards the hand that is supporting it. It indicates that the interlocutor is getting bored.

You can often see in the subject a clear sign of tiredness: eyes half closed and relaxed facial muscles.

This is a consideration gesture that expresses boredom for what you are hearing.

Touch the chin lightly: this is a clear meditation sign, the subject is about to make a decision.

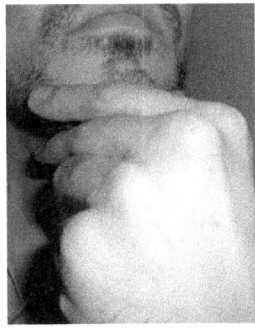

It is usually adopted when you ask an opinion about something your interlocutor is interested in.

Index finger on cheek: the hand is leaned against the cheek and the index finger usually points the eye.

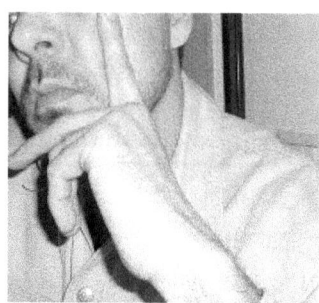

This is a negative meditation gesture because it says that the subject is sceptical about what they are hearing, and the decision they make will usually be adverse to their interlocutor. If you happen to notice this gesture, be careful to what you are saying because it is causing a critical behaviour in your interlocutor.

Index finger on temple: hand on cheek and index finger touching the temple.
It indicates a meditational behaviour but above all, it says that the interlocutor is interested in the conversation and that their opinion about it is positive.

Thumb under chin: even though it may appear that the interlocutor is interested, in reality they are not.

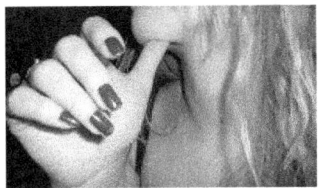

The thumb under the chin supports the head and it has the same negative meaning of boredom, as the hand supporting the head gesture.

In this chapter you could see the difference between a positive and interested evaluation. A gesture can turn into another during a conversation, for example from boredom to interest.

CHAPTER 8: EXERCISES

In this chapter I wanted to ask some simple questions to test you on what you have learnt through this handbook. You will find some questions with pictures about all the topics we have talked about. You will find the description of hypothetical sceneries, where you have to interpret the subject's body language.
You will find the answers at the end of this chapter. Analyze the context carefully, the body signs and their concordance.
If you give a wrong answer to a question, read the relevant contents again.

1) FOR MEN
You are in a club and you have just met a girl that you find very attractive. Half an hour in the conversation, she brushes off some fluffs from your collar.

Afterwards you go and sit at a table to continue the conversation. The girl is very interested in what you are saying, and while she listens to you keeping eye contact, she adopts this pose:

How does the girl feel about you? Which signs have you noticed?

2) FOR MEN

You meet a girl in a pub during an aperitif. You approach her with an excuse and you start the conversation. Her friends go towards the bar counter and she looks at them in an angry way. The woman poses like this:

What happened and what does she think about you?

3) FOR MEN
You are in a shop and you see a friend of yours with another girl. You say hello and stop for a conversation. Your friend introduces you her shopping mate. You start asking her some questions to know her better.
While the girl talks to you, she looks very sociable and adopts this position with her hips slightly tilted:

When the girl talks to you, she often shows you her left palm and she curls her hair with her right hand:

What does it mean?

4) FOR WOMEN

You are in a club and you are talking to your friend when a guy arrives and starts talking to you. You like him. During the conversation you notice that he poses like this:

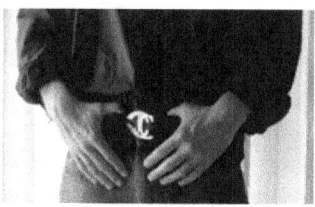

The guy keeps talking to you looking into your eyes and then he looks at your neck.

What does it mean?

5) FOR WOMEN:

You are doing some shopping in a shopping centre. The sales assistant, a good looking guy, keeps looking at you. He comes close to you and starts a conversation about a dress that you wanted to try on. The guy introduces himself shaking your hand like this:

While you continue your conversation, you notice that the guy adopts this posture:

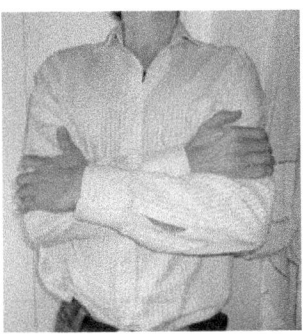

Is the guy self-confident? How does he feel about you?

6) FOR MEN:
A female colleague of yours often wants to have lunch with you. While you talk to her, you notice that she often plays with a bottle:

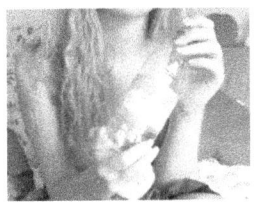

Furthermore you notice that she is sitting with her legs

crossed and she plays a lot with her shoe, taking it off and putting it on:

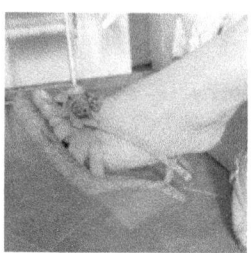

What does it mean?

7) FOR MEN

You are with a friend of yours in a pub. While she is writing a text message on her mobile phone, she stands very close to you and she often touches your chest or shoulder:

But you also notice that she often adopts this position

when she talks to you:

How does your friend feel about you?

8) FOR MEN AND WOMEN

You are at a business meeting and you notice that, as soon as you start talking, a colleague of yours moves her hand as if she wanted to clean the desk:

And while you are explaining your arguments she poses like this.

What does your colleague think about your argumentations?

9) FOR MEN AND WOMEN

If someone bites their lips like this:

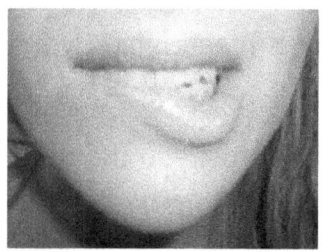

Are they attracted to you?

10) FOR MEN

You are talking to a girl you have just met and she puts the glass that she has in her hand in front of her chest:

She is obviously showing a closed attitude towards you and your conversation. How can you change her attitude into a more positive one?

11) FOR WOMEN

While you are talking to a friend of yours, you notice that he often poses like this:

You also notice that his pupils are dilated when he talks to you.

How does your friend feel about you?

12) FOR MEN AND WOMEN

You are a salesperson (B) and you have to convince your client (A) to buy your product. You are sitting at a table in these positions:

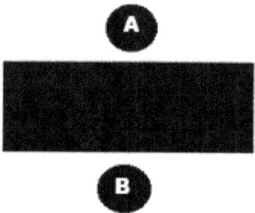

While you are talking about your product's qualities, you notice that your client sits like this:
What do you do? Do you try going closer to your client changing your seat?

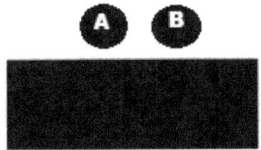

Or do you try and convince him a little more staying where you are?

13) FOR MEN AND WOMEN

A guy spends the whole night in a club keeping his hands in his pockets:

Is he self-confident?

A guy adopts this position instead:

Is he self-confident?

14) FOR MEN

You are sitting on a couch with two women, one of them sits with a leg under the other and her knee is pointing you:

What's the meaning of it, in your opinion?

15) FOR MEN AND WOMEN

A person that shakes your hand keeping his arm almost

stretched:

Why does he do that?

16) FOR MEN AND WOMEN
A girl holds her left arm with her right hand like this:

Can this be considered a closed gesture?

17) FOR MEN AND WOMEN
If someone keeps adjusting their shirt cuffs:

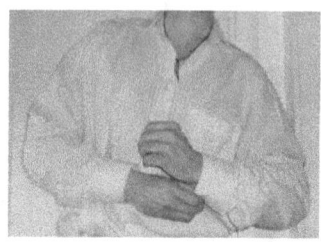

What is their emotional state?

18) FOR MEN AND WOMEN

Men's feet point the woman. The woman's left foot point outwards. Why?

19) FOR MEN AND WOMEN:

You need a favour and you are asking your friend if he

could give you a lift the day after. Your friend sits like this:

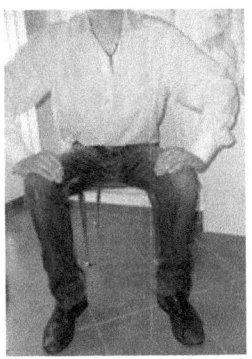

Why? Before he gives you his answer with words, do you think he will give you that lift?

20) FOR MEN AND WOMEN

Do these positions indicate a dominant or closed attitude?

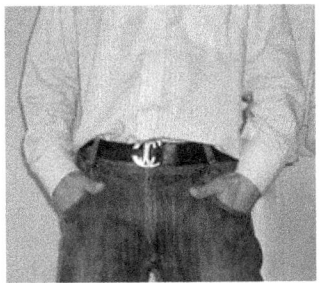

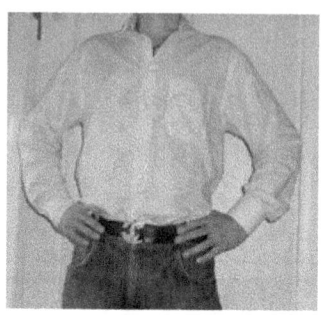

21) FOR MEN AND WOMEN

Here are three different kinds of smiles:

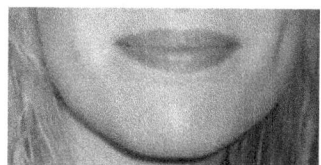

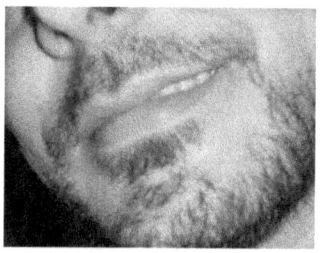

Which one of them has a positive connotation?

22) FOR MEN AND WOMEN

A student adopts this pose during an oral test:

Do you think he knows the answers to the teacher's questions?

23) FOR MEN AND WOMEN

Someone shakes your hand trying to turn your palm up. What does that mean?

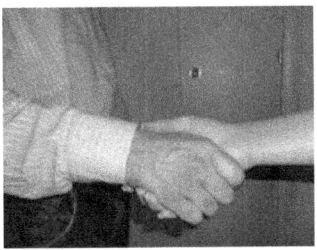

All the answers to the questions are shown below.

In these exercises you won't find all the body signs that I have explained in the books, but only the most important ones!

Practice reading body language in everyday life!

At every social occasion, try to behave so that you trigger a reaction in your interlocutor, and you will have the chance to consider the meaning of their body language.

You will notice that some people use body language more than others.

Answers:

1) They are both appreciation signs. Besides, the girl keeps eye contact with you while she speaks and this is a third sign. The woman is attracted; the seductive process should have a positive outcome.

2) The girl was involved in a conversation with her friends and your approach probably irritated her. The position she adopted with her crossed arms is a clear closed and indisposition sign. The girl considers you a bore. You started off on the wrong foot!

When you approach a woman, consider the whole situation: if she is engaged in a conversation with her friends, wait for the appropriate time to approach her.

3) The girl you have been introduced to by your friend thinks that you are attractive; she thinks that you are good looking. Suggest going shopping all together in another city to seduce her.

On that day you should try and make the girl you like feel at ease, then you will ask for her telephone number.

If you had invited only her straight away, you would have had a "no" as an answer

4) The guy probably likes you. The first position shows his openness towards you, and his look means that he is very interested

5) The guy's signals are contrasting. By shaking your hand so close to you, he shows that his personal space is small, so he may come across as a very outgoing and self-confident person. But his crossed arms say that he is nervous. There can be two explanations for that: either the conversation irritated him, or he is showing a fake self-confidence. When you see contrasting signals, you should analyze the context and wait for other body signs.

6) Your colleague is clearly attracted to you: these are two signs that have a sexual connotation; she likes you very much.

7) This situation shows two contrasting body signals: the

first may indicate that your friend is interested; the second indicates a partial closed attitude. Women usually become very confidential with their friends, and they tend to touch them; but if they notice advances from your side, they could get defensive. Your friend probably knows that you could misunderstand her behaviour and she gets defensive to make you understand that.

8) By moving her hand on the desk, your colleague is expressing rejection towards what you are saying. The second position shows that she feels nervous and strongly insecure. She probably felt she was involved in your speech in a negative way; or you irritate her with your behaviour at work.

9) Probably not! She feels nervous and anxious when she is with you. Wait for other gestures or positions to confirm that, because she may just only be very shy.

10) First of all try not to invade her personal space. Use many openness gestures -like showing your palms- then with your words, try to make her feel at ease.

11) Your friend probably feels something more than a friendship towards you. By showing you his muscles he wants to court you and his pupils' dilation -unless it's caused by the light - expresses a strong interest.

12) Don't move and try to convince your client. His closure position indicates criticism towards your argumentations. In this context, if you adopt a friendly position you will be likely to push him away.

13) He probably isn't: hiding his hands indicates that he is insecure, his rejection for the environment he is in, and for any kind of approach by others. Only his further closed gestures can confirm this. The second guy, instead, tries to affirm a dominant state.

14) The girl is probably attracted to you. Wait for other appreciation signs to be sure.

15) They are probably doing it because they need a large personal space, and by keeping their arm during their handshake, they want to stay at a safe distance.

16) Yes! Because it's a gesture that is linked to a stressful situation.

17) It's a stressful situation, or this person feels uncomfortable

18) Probably because the woman is not enjoying the

situation and she wants to leave

19) Your friend thinks the conversation is over and he wants to stand up. As soon as he is up he will probably say that he accepts your request.

20) Dominance. The first one expresses a strong self-confidence; the second one expresses a "territorial" defence.

21) The second one is a positive and honest smile because it involves both lips and eyes; the other two have a negative meaning:

22) He/she probably knows the answers. The student shows that he/she is self-confident and that he/she has a solution to a specific problem.

23) He/she wants to subjugate you by imposing his/her dominant state. The handshake is very energetic and the interlocutor will try to turn your palm up.

CHAPTER 9: CONCLUSION

Here we are at the conclusion. For further readings about seduction and about psychology applied to seduction I suggest that you read the following e-books:

- How to attract and seduce women with the secrets of italian latin lover – Davide Balesi.

- 12 Approcci vincenti – Davide Balesi.

- 5 motivi per cui non piaci alle donne – Davide Balesi and Alessio Maffei.

- L'enciclopedia della seduzione – Davide Balesi.

- L'enciclopedia della seduzione versione cartacea – Davide Balesi and Alessio Maffei (Published by Youcanprint).

All E-books from LifeLace Editions catalogue:

http://lifelaceeditions.blogspot.it/p/catalogo-ebook_3.html

Thank you, Davide Balesi

###